I'LL RETURN

AN ANTHOLOGY OF POEMS

AANCHAL MUNJAL

Copyright © Aanchal Munjal
All Rights Reserved.

This book has been self-published with all reasonable efforts taken to make the material error-free by the author. No part of this book shall be used, reproduced in any manner whatsoever without written permission from the author, except in the case of brief quotations embodied in critical articles and reviews.

The Author of this book is solely responsible and liable for its content including but not limited to the views, representations, descriptions, statements, information, opinions and references ["Content"]. The Content of this book shall not constitute or be construed or deemed to reflect the opinion or expression of the Publisher or Editor. Neither the Publisher nor Editor endorse or approve the Content of this book or guarantee the reliability, accuracy or completeness of the Content published herein and do not make any representations or warranties of any kind, express or implied, including but not limited to the implied warranties of merchantability, fitness for a particular purpose. The Publisher and Editor shall not be liable whatsoever for any errors, omissions, whether such errors or omissions result from negligence, accident, or any other cause or claims for loss or damages of any kind, including without limitation, indirect or consequential loss or damage arising out of use, inability to use, or about the reliability, accuracy or sufficiency of the information contained in this book.

Made with ❤ on the Notion Press Platform
www.notionpress.com

To my husband

who always believes in me.

Contents

Foreword   *ix*

Preface   *xi*

Acknowledgements   *xiii*

1. Prelude   1

2. The Poet And The Poem   2

3. I   3

4. Addressal-1   4

5. Addressal -2   5

6. Sighs   6

7. Life   7

8. Unrighteous Endeavour   8

9. Fortune   9

10. Not An Adult   10

11. To Seize   12

12. God   14

13. I'll Return   16

14. Thy In Thy   18

15. Satisfaction   19

16. Support   20

17. City One (part -1)   21

18. (part -2)   22

19. Illusive Worlds   23

20. Self - Realization   24

21. The Work Is Persisting   26

22. He Is Alive   28

23. Scepticism   30

Contents

24. Swift More Swift — 31

25. Friends — 33

26. Gaining Or Losing — 34

27. If That Occurred — 35

28. Lesser But — 36

29. Over Competition — 37

30. Jai Hind — 38

31. Acceptance- Accord — 39

32. Stuck Badly — 41

33. Birth — 43

34. Poem — 44

35. Contemplation — 45

36. Concurrence — 46

37. Reasonably Futile — 47

38. Justice- Injustice — 48

39. A Narrative Poem — 50

40. Lovingly — 52

41. Droplets Of Dew — 53

42. Undoubtedly — 54

43. Mishap — 56

44. Politics — 57

45. Irony — 58

46. The Third One — 59

47. Obstacles — 60

48. Confined — 61

49. Home — 62

Contents

50. Inspiration   64

51. I Was The River   65

52. Spiritual (sep 11, New York)   66

53. But Still A Difference   68

54. Vacant Place   70

55. Damaged Roads, Glittering Cars   72

56. Everyone Was Immigrant   73

57. City Vs Village   74

58. In My Rajasthan   75

59. Fanaticism   76

60. Butterflies   77

61. Departing From Here   79

62. One Secret   80

63. Struggle   81

64. I Started Liking Her   82

65. Prayer   83

66. Desires   84

EVOKE

67. ….. At Last   87

68. Certainty In Uncertainty   88

69. No One………who Wandered   90

70. The House Speaks   91

71. Roof   93

72. Oh! Regret?   95

73. Cheat   97

74. Two Girls   98

Contents

75. House: Ours Or Rented….   100

76. Apology   101

77. Its Morning   102

78. A Statement: Not A Poem   104

79. Reality Of Dreams – Life Or Reality Of Life – A Dream   105

80. Need   106

81. Thy Be Lord Krishna   107

82. It Is Life   109

83. Inchmeal   110

84. On Being Women   111

85. Did The World Change?   112

86. Introspection   113

87. The First Human   115

88. The One   117

89. I And The Labourer   119

90. Evoke   120

Foreword

Translation undoubtedly gives a broader audience a chance to perceive the literature differently. It also provides an opportunity to be recognized and understood by readers. Initially, I thought to concentrate more on reading and writing but later, my interest developed in poetry and prose. So, I started writing poetry and a few pieces of prose during my adolescent years, and this initial thought of writing extended to the whole journey to date. As I am an introvert, I never thought to bring my work of literature in front of the public. However, Aanchal's efforts made me complacent that my work would be translated and the book would reach a broader audience.

Meeting Ms. Aanchal raised hope that having my work translated may take my writings to the next platform. It was her sincerity and commitment, which assured me that she could complete this task. She gradually evolved herself and translated fantastically. I hope in the future, she will thrive more and more. I heartily wish for her good health, spirits, and interest. I am indebted to her that she spent her time understanding my poems and translating them into English.

Best Regards

Dr. Manish Goswami

Professor Pharma Sciences

Saraswati Group of Colleges

Gharuan, Mohali, India

Pin Code: 140413

goswamidrmanish@gmail.com

91-9872262777

Preface

"I'll return" is an anthology of two poetry books, 'Do Ladkiyaan' (Two Girls) and 'Main Phir Aaunga' (I'll Return), originally written in the Hindi Language by Dr. Manish Goswami. He started writing these poems during his adolescent age while struggling to establish his career. At that time, he was conscious of achieving a higher purpose and meaning in life. It worked as a survival instinct for him. The poet found peace in writing poetry while achieving academic excellence. Through his poems, he was able to voice his internal conflicts.

Dr. Goswami feels that poetry can help fill the void in people's lives. We generally use antidepressants, mobile phones, and television to relieve stress. However, poetry has served the same purpose from ancient to modern times.

In Dr. Goswami's poems, there is a tinge of Indian life as he mentions "revolving spoke in his poem "Life." However, the expression "revolving spoke" signifies the ordinary person's struggles in India. The following lines illustrate the same:

Thriving the spinning wheel

in the course of life, revolving spoke.

A heart -

a tiny piece of paper entangled and engulfed

....

Lust and mirage, a thorn in the flesh, yearned to elude.

Besides the poem mentioned above, certain poems have an entirely different stance, as in "Addressal-2". In this poem, the poet personifies "Smile' and directly asks questions to her.

Such personification helps us to understand an entirely different perspective of poetry.

Smile

If I drag you on lips

Idly,

Will you sink

in the bottom of my heart?

Like the unfathomable rays in the reservoir.

Will vitalize the entirety, plants, animals,

earth and water.....

When flowers, leaves, eggs, and bubbles

emerge on the surface.......

Will utter

how ecstatic the surface (the inner self) is.

Hence, the reader should read the poems by himself, explore an entirely different world of poetry, and fill the void in her life through a new experience of literature.

By:

Aanchal Munjal

Assistant Professor

Saraswati Group of Colleges

Gharuan, Mohali, Punjab

India, Pin Code: 140413

Email: aanchal2502@gmail.com

Contact No: 9781999154

Acknowledgements

Everyone wants to grow in one's professional and personal life. And my professional life grew under the guidance of Dr. Manish Goswami. He ignited the spark of writing in me and showed me a new and unexplored direction. I offer my sincere appreciation for the learning opportunities provided by him.

On the other side, my personal life flourished with the support of my husband, Gunjan. He is my friend and life support. Without his encouragement, this book couldn't have been completed. I extend special thanks to him because he trusted my capabilities and potential, which remained unrecognized before I met him.

Regards
Aanchal Munjal

1. Prelude

Time & again,
I discern
the poem is undesired;
it has professed a lot
and now life is shrinked
by virtue of it.
At last,
the soaring luminous light
and grandeur in the darkness
akin to life that evolves poems.
Time and again,
when many poems contrived,
it seemed
life is prolonged and
pledged to confess
emptiness is not everlasting
nor the existence of darkness
nor the verge of life .....

2. The poet and the poem

I yearned to be a human first
thereupon a poet.
Needless the poems to emerge as a poet.
Every poem is a lyric,
Not every lyric-a poem,
still, a poet fathoms every lyric.
Witnessed many poets who don't chant poems?
Unfathomed
Which poet- Am I?
A Minstrel- who recites the poem, or the one,
never gives utterance to poems
Or the poet, who truly avow and enacts the poem.

3. I

Burst too high in the sky,
the bottle rocket bestows
immense ecstasy and zeal to the owner.
Shaping myself thereafter besprinkled,
The mere motive of embracing the sky creator,
thy feel the akin ecstasy of owner ....
...........................thy sky

thy shine

thy radiance

last, in essence, forever.

4. Addressal-1

Grief
If I subsist joyfully turning a blind eye
heedless! Imprudent!
The Sun that doesn't see the night,
Will you resign?
Like the darkness
or you yourself were nothing.
Defined or disdained by us,
then how you became autonomous.

5. Addressal -2

Smile
If 'I drag you on lips Idly.'
Will you sink
into the bottom of my heart?
Like the unfathomable rays in the reservoir.
Will vitalize entirety plants, animals,
earth and water.....
When flowers, leaves, eggs, and bubbles
emerge on the surface.....
Will utter
how ecstatic the surface (the inner self) is.

6. Sighs

Heaving a sigh with vigor
for eternity
every now and then to survive.
Can hear the voice delved into the bottom saying-
Thou, just thou remain by any means.............
Amid
the gradual intense sigh-
Like an island discovered in the storm,
Perchance the spine of a whale, either real or fictitious.
The question?
Were breaths created to give us life,
or were we created to make breaths?
Still, the mere last evidence of life.......
When gradual sighs fade away forever,
then everyone will profess wow! Lived a long life.

7. Life

Thriving the spinning wheel
in the course of life, revolving spoke.
A heart -
a tiny piece of paper
entangled and engulfed
when blows the fast wind
Till when? Till when?
Lust and mirage,
a thorn in the flesh,
yearned to elude.
Elated heart! Full of mirth?
Wind! Wind! Sky! Sky!
ceased the car
rested the paper
shade of dilemma
unwavering........ serene...... poised
as the destination arrived.

8. Unrighteous Endeavour

An agitated child plunged
the flying airplane by throwing a pebble,
implausible, meaningless,
yet an unrighteous endeavor,
in our vicinity
on us,
by others, even by the neighboring nations
premeditated profound thoughts time and again.
Reason-
the grass is always greener
on the other side of the fence.
Resentment, dissatisfaction with himself,
seizing the paddles, sinking the entire boat,
then himself submerged weeping,
recollecting the sweet memories of past
but who brought the present?

9. Fortune

The line on the hands gets altered
with the present for the future.
Thereupon remained still
by taking the imprint of the past
creates disappointments when seen by eyes
vain as reminiscence in the present.

10. Not an Adult

Though with them and grew up
yet a child, they profess not an adult.
An eternal static smile on face............
can't laugh senselessly met with great vigor
but not appraised as cordial because not an adult.
Still pristine and elated, no lines on the forehead.
Can see with open eyes
the sky replete with hopes.
Though can see something in someone
but not an adult.
Just going to reach the destination
while walking,
swayed yet slithers
can't forge ahead
while resting on someone's back
didn't flourish
because not an adult.
Moving like a small child the way I am
free-spirited, nothing disguised or enshrouded.
A small child in the crowd
won't get trampled under the feet of adults
or myself become
an adult and crush someone else.
or create an adult
Who tramples someone else........

Filled with fear as not an adult.

11. To Seize

To seize for self-possession, then,
hastily unleash
a transient enticement,
a swift vigorous endeavor,
an enormous wave
that can accumulate in a second,
anything emerged from
the internal chaos in the second bizarre avarice,
yearning to blend swiftly,
to gain enormously in abundance
and dismay the untiring,
perpetual small waves
but by degrees
the emerging wave from the sea,
gushing with time
quarreling with wind
unraveling and discerning
when reaching the banks
will offer a small gift to beloved(bank)
will all swayed in mirth- by the drenched soil
by the pure wind, the blossomed leaves…
even when submerged
the profound sweet memories till when?
By the time the ocean sustains
essence – till the Universe…..thence eternally.

While accumulating
the same enormous wave, again submerged and
in abundance, to accumulate the sum ………
………covetous….. unidentified.

12. God

Some shrewd, some atheists or devotees
as said, everyone has a barren center of faith
in this spirited world voiced itself
conceived itself
the proof of truth.
Erects the tree that bowed of values,
as branches bow the burden of fruits.
Thus in the race of touching the zenith of the sky
Do the trees hold back?
This is the outcome of imagination
one pretence
and one submission
one means of self–satisfaction.
A ground
to emerge again
to ravage, seize and pounce afterward, the solution
of proving oneself innocent.
This is God
believed by all,
by preference magnanimous,
benevolent, and bestowing wishes.
Some offer ample love
by butchering the living
to dead.
Some receive the self-reliance

by ignoring the rest of the animate, create
restrained, uncompassionate, and lifeless society.

13. I'll return

Highs and lows wax and wane
intermittent stride, incessant flow
after completing the journey,
I'll return
I'll return.
In the fragrant flowers of besprinkled plants,
plunged in the sweetness of laden trees
I'll return.
By demolishing the indigence,
will become the smile of feeble,
by gaining perpetually
will disseminate
with time will scatter
in the varied colors
will bring one shine.
I will return
by becoming the disciple of the paradigm,
the admirer of truth
will submerge in the utterance of truth.
I'll return by becoming the vigor in
the utterance of the disciple,
become glorious
in the sweat of son
vanished and emerged in a second, I'll return.
Evidently, materialize in new form replenish,

revived and refined
will shroud in earthly to unearthly
I'll return.
Clouds to rain, rain to streams,
thereupon become the ocean,
I, nor vanished nor adrift
I become reincarnated time & again
went to become pristine, I'll return.

14. Thy in Thy

Thy becomes- Someone else, for thyself.
Like merging clouds will forget everything
from where thy commenced, how much wearied,
how many strikes endured, agitated, agonized.........
and thereupon
will not be glanced then, everyone asks
Where did thy go?
Where did thy go?

15. Satisfaction

Most drudgery is performed
as- buttermilk and butter from milk.
One prolonged labor
mingled in the stomach
-still the same milk
-one goal.
Path of Karma inspired by the
a glimpse of life.
Result - one profound satisfaction.
Why didn't the milk gulp down precedently?
Everything swathed and submerged
in one essence, the vitality
to discern the seven colors in the white rays of the Sun,
then the indefinite self-satisfaction
sensed every second of every moment- that "life is a gift."
God is prayer
"For all bestow some milk And one ray of Sun."
Thy becomes- Someone else, for thyself.
Like merging clouds will forget everything
from where thy commenced, how much wearied,
how many strikes endured, agitated, agonized.........
and thereupon
will not be glanced then, everyone asks
Where did thy go?
Where did thy go?

16. Support

A little reclusive at home
ran in the crowd from solitude like a thirsty.
In the pursuit of water,
glanced all around the crowd, astonished,
discerned like,
the water of the ocean
able to behold but can not drink.
In apprehension ran from the crowd
speechless- at home.
A man standing in a calendar
seems like us voiced-
"Where have you vanished- for many days."
Was sitting- close-lipped replied inwardly
"just like that."

17. City one (part -1)

Thy confines are discernible
as thou are meager.
Ever vigilant of the occurrence of something momentous,
considering the abundance of boundaries
but, yet, a lot less.
In the conspicuous boundaries,
I derive favor from someone;
sometimes to accomplish
small goals to fulfill big goals.
I sail across boundaries to discern
some colossal boundless confines
to bestow you something
when return.
As thy are tree
And I —the adrift root I enslaved
by this sense of enlightenment,
I feel complacent -
Tree, thou should not wither/perish city,
thou shouldn't flourish.

18. (Part -2)

Coming from varied villages,
the inhabitants took land in one place
(and inhabited a quiet gigantic orderly –city.)
Drifting from divergent villages,
these inhabitants greet as city dwellers,
very formally, intellectually,
and as inhabitants from varied villages.
The city dwellers embrace the villagers of their own village
in the city as the countrymen.
When they reached the village,
the city dwellers condemned the town folks.
Some countrymen striving
to settle down in the city, finding land
amongst their countrymen
as city dwellers are atrocious.

19. Illusive worlds

The world —an illusion entirely,
even Einstein could prove
but, foretime rested in peace.
In a dream,
the confines of the mind ceased ahead of time.
And, kept us bewildered, what is it all?
Then, we become the characters of our own dreams.
Destiny-the director,
Producer- the nature.
The director himself evolves the character,
by the fingers of opportunities
emerges from situations and circumstances;
hence, everyone's life gets distinctive
even though made on the same potter's wheel
with the same soil.
Someone's pleasant,
someone's horrified
or someone's fragmented
amidst- just now shattered
just now shattered.

20. Self - realization

A Man
is getting filthy with age
like a stream
as it flows
tainted by surroundings,
change its colors
while advancing.
Water-
Thy are immortal
for stream- essence soul-
-as it seems- thou
too get transformed
so pure in childhood just emerged from the origin,
progressed a bit from splendid colossal mountains to downhill.
While progressing,
recollect the evergreen memories of mountains
and golden clouds, as nothing will be
in reminiscence onwards thence,
progress mindlessly.
Yet, looking back
at the origin-
the childhood memories.
But, a question-
persist even after getting so filthy;
why is it persistent?

So, enunciate
Why thou so pure earlier
should remain filthy by origin- water (soul).
Why entail values? Why need preaching?
Soul, thou remain filthy would not be mindful
what is good,
nor necessitate to fathom.
All rejoiced in remaining filthy……?

21. The work is persisting

Developing a paunch
becoming the patients
devouring the medicines
swallowing the sweets
the work is booming
the work is persisting.
Investing in lottery
making fools
spoiling the fortune
sleeping as starved
clinging to the dreams,
the work is persisting.
The bus is devastating;
all are climbing,
emissing the fumes
heaving breaths
just heart is beating;
the work is persisting.
The queue is increasing
offering the bribe
the police are witnessing
taking part
the number is nearing
the work is persisting
Samosas are frying

research is enriching
the class is bustling
the exams are operating
the college is functioning
the work is persisting.
Burglary is booming
hoarding money
portents are occurring
feeling frightened
donating to charity virtuousness is booming
the work is persisting.
The nation is blazing, yet,
progressing pride is withering
still bragging about gaining debts
the work is persisting.

22. He is alive

He can behold
He can listen
He gulps the water
thereupon flows through pores.
His hands toil ceaselessly,
surpassing the machine
as even a machine requires a mechanic.
He himself is the machine or the mechanic.
He covertly builds a house
like a bird builds a nest
in the casement of someone,
Oh! Unknowing when the owner catches sight.
Entirety, the proof perhaps,
at times he feels-
that he is faintly alive.
Now and then, dilapidated.
Why is he like this?
At times conflicting thoughts (he isn't like that)
then leaving all thoughts behind
becoming a hanging leaf
on the spider web.
Initially revolving clockwise,
Thereupon anticlockwise- a mere process
unceasing
recurring a machine

indeed, he is a mechanical creation,
yet, bewildered
just one testament staunch eternal......
Death which validates -he was alive.

23. Scepticism

Tomorrow,
where I am proceeding,
won't be my path – of destination to attain- unprolific futile.
Will all my drudgery go in vain?
Or to take a pertinent path by turning around?
Were those winds of adversity in the past?
The winds- the tides of time
where they were dragging
driven in that direction- to be saved
from getting scattered like straws.
or, while advancing idly instantly rushed
under the thatch
to be saved from rain.
When the rain ceased,
I discerned it was dusk.
Oh! a new beginning once again.
Essence, either learn to remain futile
or selfless lesson of work
or fathom this metaphysical world.

24. Swift more swift

The moment
regained consciousness,
glanced all sides
in cognizance fathomed-
be dressed in the shoes of maturity
and run swift, swifter.
But, when veins were the same,
the same blood
the same cells
and the same air outside
the same precise quantity of oxygen.
The same precise molecules
of carbohydrates, protein,
fat in food, then,
all stagnated by virtue of it.
How?
Because in relativity,
the race is identical
on the ground of
maximum equivalent energy,
so everyone glancing
at each other as stagnant.
Such as even the voice of gasping a root process.
Tranquility, an unwavering situation-
What a predicament!

By crossing countless births & lives,
God bestowed this prize.
Undefined, laden with a dignified style of varied disparities
gentle sensation subtle as water, delicate as a flower
enchantment of moonlight,
the fierceness of the sun robustness of the mountain
-What wasn't offered?
But, ran like the way everything got trivial
and unaware of what lags,
so running swift more swift.

25. Friends

Friends
I have a long list of perpetual names,
one after another
I am accustomed,
but as others,
thy be deemed smaller,
being stated in the list?
Granting a name of words to yourself.........
just Elections are ahead of
the worldly achievements
and the unworldly alliance.

26. Gaining or Losing

Jubilant whistle
Gaining or Losing
whilst gaining and progressing,
to attain more yet, (indelibrately)
loose whilst attaining and progressing
but not reasoned as
losing after attaining.
That's the difference
between heading with Karma
or receiving with destiny.
In the course of progression,
for not procuring to the maximum ability-
is a notion of apprehension.
By virtue of Karma,
will procure in abundance.
Nothing was lost
what we were deprived of had no experience of that.
So, substantially felt no repentance.
Ample experiences here,
and this happens to be one lakh
one still, remorseful essence
the false melancholy.

27. If that occurred

When contemplate
if walked more straight would attain
which didn't acquire still,
got in abundance,
yet insufficient,
reasoned as maximum -of efforts.
Still a difference
between not procured in the fullness
or attaining finite.
Essence,
void of that experience
when gained nothing.
what happened then
inside or outside the world?
when you were renounced
.... and whatnot.
Oh! delightedly
still not outside the game,
not cowardliness
nor the symbol of standstill,
but the birth of contentment.

28. Lesser but

Expenditure of one hundred
but splurged one thousand
require one hundred fifty
but encashed five hundred
urged a little but dissipated the entire life.

29. Over Competition

"Not less than others,"
they intended to divulge
others discerned and
apprised differently like them.
"We also not less than others."
All ignorant if
anyone had in abundance.
"Not in the state of inferiority."
The pretence reinforced
in expressing, apprising, and feigning.

30. Jai Hind

Some hands raised
or lifted a clenched fist in fervor
"to uplift the nation," uttered or voiced.
Some hands unstated covertly on purpose
"that nation has wiped out from earth"
proceed in this fashion.
Some people two
or four inclined
"to offer shoulders"
forged ahead-
by degrees.

31. Acceptance- Accord

Friend, gentleman! -Monsieur!
Now can fathom thy talk.
It didn't occur that
I wasn't in the ocean
where the waves of feelings
along with the low and high tides,
where at times, the winds blow to ignite.
This, too, didn't occur on the boat
on which I was sailing and advancing its oar
was in others' hands and now only in mine,
that I have to determine the direction.
Even earlier, the oar itself created the space
by the flow of opportunities, but now perhaps
I am heading the boat.
Only I will give it the complete direction.
The direction that
may influence the direction of others.
Some riders or some sailors behind.
Yes- I need to complete this voyage
clenching the oar in fist,
undeviating neck
straight ahead- towards the goal.
By these
I fathom thy talk.
Though not the complete reason itself.

Essence,
I got too stuck
in the web-like thee.
Our webs are weaved differently even if
thy visualizing in thy way and I in mine
to fathom the orientation of the knot of life.
Thy discern the difference
as I just got stuck now
and thy long ago.
Heaven knows what they uttered
and remained speechless
for not getting any reaction.
Might contemplate,
what is the benefit
neither I will discern thou inner world
nor thy will give it
worldly form-word and sentence.
So, silence is justified.
At least, I discerned what thy thought.
Yet, when we both emerge from these webs separately,
will be more elevated than in the past.
Neither any spider would approach,
nor it weaves the web;
even if someone weaves,
our stature will be gigantic.
In this hope
I professed all...........
in the endeavor to see one light
.... Kindest regards.

32. Stuck Badly

Some people
mused to be fit as a fiddle
ate in abundance died
as adulteration was high.
Some thought to be fit,
jogged
knocked down
as traffic was high.
Some contemplate this to be
delusive and unsubstantial
they thought unconventionally
became insane
as confusion was high.
Some discovered
the significance of life in love.
They discerned the world
in the gleaming eyes of their beloved,
became lovers,
then flopped
as infatuation was high.
Some perceived
it to be the culture of the forest
became virtuous
get robbed
as corruption was high.

Some glanced
at everyone and compiled everything
created one poem
and themselves become 'a poet'.

33. Birth

Affixed at times
after getting shattered.
Confined unreasonably
or gradually
just assembled,
to subjoin
mindful of being shattered
yet cognizant -Thy has to be kept healthy.
Conscious now, it seems
thy different from animals,
if thy have not scratched the pole
not roared
not snatched.
This is the period of gestation,
in this enlarged womb, shortly,
there will be a mirthful human being.

34. Poem

At times, the income increased
at times, the expenditure
at times, I ceased thereupon proceed
at times, the path advanced
at times, the destination
a mirage amidst,
ceaselessly persisted was my poem – Unwavering.

35. Contemplation

Shifting from
this house to others
living in varied cities from hand to mouth,
toiled unremittingly to earn butter on stale bread.
From dawn to dusk
dusk to dawn
in this monotony refashioned a little.
Neither I discern not thy fathom
whilst turning back, one could witness.
Bounteous heads, bounteous brains, empty hearts,
and higher dreams gratify somewhat amidst all.
Desert this world abandon the problems
return to the old street by wrenching everything.

36. Concurrence

If we presume
we have dissension
on varied things
from one-another
essence we have perfect concurrence.

37. Reasonably Futile

Villages intend to be towns

that themselves intend to be a city.

A city dreams of being a district,

A district intends to see itself as a metropolitan city.

Half of the population

the metropolitan city intends to go to - village.

Many people in metropolitan

cities moved from villages

by walking through these villages, towns, and cities.

Yearn to be

a newspaper

reached to all,

acclaimed even its frontispiece

be the paramount

many remained bestselling reached to everyone..........

...........gained recognition.

The next morning.............

..............were forgotten.

The next month.............

.... were gone in scrap

and yet.....................

..................misconceived

that remained victorious in this life.

38. Justice- Injustice

After the journey from the earth to the sky,
both were kept in the same section
-the one collecting the garbage
-the other accumulating wealth.
Reason
their achievements
-heaps of papers- were alike.
These are akin to heaps,
but variations in
-accruement-
one in the 'rubbish.'
another 'in the beautiful four confines of metal.'
A little later, the first troop
(collector of garbage) arranged to be sent
to paradise expeditiously,
the other batch was already agitated
(as they were not asked for tea or water till now)
Reason
both had an entirely different approach
to collect the garbage.
-For one
by putting his blood, sweat, and tears
in the scorching heat.
-For others
by enslaving others to

put blood, sweat, and tears in the scorching heat.

39. A Narrative Poem

Once upon a time,
when there was life on a planet in
this Universe.
Life is identical to the transition
if enormously flourished
even the adjacent planets
put efforts into approaching it.
But heaven knows this transition
is the gift by whom?
Congenial, delightful, and meaningful,
that one planet had life.
At every moment, millions of people
agitated about their existence.
Even the affluent were perturbed.
Amongst them, there were some
who were more distressed about their poem
then their own self.
Both groups
were hilarious for each other.
Perhaps, after the transition of life,
the poem, too, has its transition.
Among the ideologist of poetry,
some created a poem
by being enraptured
by their love for poetry,

some ideologists read it.
Generations of ideologists got old and
the second transition of the poem
after this life
became speckless
like the grass of plains in summers
sand, just sand.
That the rain
of the new generation has fallen,
someone created a poem
like growing grass in a small corner,
some wanderers glanced through it
and came to know,
one group was perturbed
- about the poem.
This remained unremitting;
the planet kept on revolving
the flow of life persisted,
and the poem kept on being created.

40. Lovingly

Our passages, our mistakes,
our destinations are divergent
varied happiness, varied sorrows, yet the same God!
Thy life, my life, diverse from one another,
my wishes, my own heart,
even though obsessed with thee.
A little pale was my face, a little pale yours
both had parted hearts, now a little united.
Neither I fathom nor thy discern,
whose flaw was it that I have or thy too
now thy affirm.

41. Droplets of Dew

The droplets of dew vanish
by the warmth of the Sun at daybreak.
Heaven knows
where are these droplets of dew?
It seems it won't ever take birth
as those virtues......
that drifts away
by promising the inner self.
Won't ever return
won't make thy worthless
by keeping upright
in this chaotic world...
At dawn, again
these gleaming droplets of dew
heaven knows
now and then, from where
they appear - the droplets of dew.

42. Undoubtedly

Certainly, it seems
that even by being the water of a ditch,
I am getting overambitious
by keeping the destiny, aspirations,
and the culmination of river
(my unison too be sublime)
Perhaps only gasping; that
I, the same substance flowing (in the river) in it.
Oh! even being aware of
I can't discern
(Heaven knows whom?)
that I entirely fathom
thy in the real sense.
When I was fragmented (the water of the ditch),
Why did I get stuck?
God! Thy can't be so mean.
Got stuck
in the same confine of a circle pondered
suffocated, at times contemplating
...........at times neutral, at times turbulent
...........but surprisingly
...........now restful, Perhaps, at times, things get clear
without the words being uttered, as everything is evident.
On the peak of the mountain
by reaching it through one step...

Just as a sapling......
my frustration, couldn't realize
when I traversed
the mountains of inferiority
and submissively
a flower floating on the bank uttered-
See! We are so complete,
though thy emerge from the river like a wave,
came alone here now we are thy companion.
I glanced at this completeness a little now
And a little advancing
that fulfills life in nullity.
Though it is united with the said beloved
but the earth in its surroundings is still barren and saline.

43. Mishap

Outside the city
on the roadside in garages
collide trees in pits
lying unknowingly ramshackle and tumbled down
truck, car, the bus as the worthless toys of a child,
threw outside the house or in the trash,
or someone created them by imitating the toys of a child.
But at least contemplate
toys in the tiny hands
overly dragged, then driven in the trash,
but those lying outside the city among them
how many were children, adults, and their elders......

44. Politics

On a moonlit night, darkness befalls
as the night commences, 'Amavasya' emerge
the politics arise in politics,
the policy of sovereignty became delusive.

45. Irony

On roads with ease
the cars and jeeps move
and collide
the cycles with one another.

46. The Third one

Those who confined in conscience entrapped in shackles
those who left behind were not fugitives
turned into bull static in the market
when walked, even the police stepped aside.
Those who went to enquire captured in crimes
those who robbed became the doorkeeper.
Some third emerged, grabbed the prize
those who toiled kept on toiling
in respect of others
by keeping garland in hands........
They just longed to conjoin
time and again
after being shattered,
how long could anyone break
conjoined time and again
after being shattered
became mercury.
How long someone is alive
with the clever intentions
those who toiled kept alive
in their endeavors forever........

47. Obstacles

*Obstacles were passing
as such, one gets old
the new one arrives.*

48. Confined

Looking for something beyond the stars
new life, new planet, new home........
And, there are some not even crossed
the confines of four walls
in their own selfishness even now.

49. Home

First
I am eager to go home.
Second
Argh! Does heaven know when I reach home?
Third,
now I proceed
by taking my home along with me
no traveler, a wanderer.
Fourth,
when no confines of troubles were there
I contemplate,
now I need to reach home.
A traveler standing for quite a long
in a train
the station is just drawing near
thereupon the home.
As time went on,
the spirit of
Vasudhaiva kutumbakam changed the time,
but then felt nostalgic about the home
seems any minute now
as a child studying in school
(who will play a lot in the evening)
thereupon go home.
When standing in the house, discerned,

in a little while
home will be built,
thereupon go home.
Later, I came outside and saw
each man
coming out of his home
to reach his own home........
(Vasudhaiva kutumbakam -a Sanskrit phrase that means
"the world is one family")

50. Inspiration

Beholding alive carcasses
I, too, stood up.

51. I was the River

Part one:
I was the river
to merge with the ocean moved relentlessly,
those who standstill didn't appreciate it
many intend to stifle me
but I was - the river.
Part Two:
He ceased me
I stopped this time, but the water
kept on flowing inside me,
I remained standstill water kept on running.
I proceeded to blend with the ocean
and become the ocean.

52. Spiritual (Sep 11, New York)

If a thousand miles away,
a stranger still buried
won't trouble our sleep
at all though our heart is sorrowful for a while.
But that day,
my sleep was perturbed
the whole night,
The first time,
I got to know myself that "I, too, am sensitive."
I contemplate it over and over that night,
One airplane after the other
Alas! Are there still some buried?
Besides the one reduced to ashes,
oh! Is there some half-burnt?
The one who did it as a mischievous boy.
By lighting the chaff,
the child remained quiet at once.
When through the chaff to the field,
field to the barn,
from one barn to another,
thereupon the entire village was burnt.
Someone asked, who did it?
The child didn't contemplate
it would be an enormous havoc

the child walked quietly.
One plane after the other slammed into the building.
The one who did it
Not sure that the entire building will collapse.
He walked unuttered as a child.
The next morning,
God felt ashamed
and stood in front of Jesus, Budh, and deities groundlessly.
He said, "There might be some lackings in my teaching."
The one who did it stood pretentiously
because he wasn't God.
Neither God nor human beings
would learn a lesson from him.

53. But still a difference

Though Gujrat and Bihar
are in the same nation
still a huge difference,
if Gujrat becomes entirely filthy,
it won't be Bihar.
Gujrat and Newyork are on the same planet
but still a difference;
if something happens in Gujrat
no attack will occur elsewhere.
And, in Newyork
if something happens,
people won't reach for the sake of votes
like vultures
to eat the carcasses.
Both Gujrat and Kashmir
are entirely different varied religions
to be kept in itself, along with equality,
in Gujrat
millions of people in one community
don't evade Gujrat like the one who evades Kashmir.
In Gujrat and
Delhi, there are refugee camps
but still, a difference.
There are camps in Gujrat to make people
feel the sense of companionship no one has left

by going elsewhere, like the camps in Delhi.
Essence
don't perceive Gujrat as India;
perceive it as Gujrat because
Gujrat is a bit different.

54. Vacant Place

There will be no vacant place
if something is vacant,
it will be the ground, not the place.
At times,
I won't rest
at some vacant place,
though,
I wished
by keeping myself aside from my place.
Many sons inherit the
vacant place of their father
fortunate than those
who kept on looking for an empty place
to let their fathers rest.....
Either increase the rent
or keep this place vacant after I left
the place, remained uninhabited for months.
As keeping the house inhabits like this
make it feel abandoned always.
Our emptiness in it could create thy place
if not filled to the brim that overflew for no reason
thou being emptied,
as such couldn't create any place in it.
He left as such
that vacant place

remained irreplaceable for years.....

55. Damaged roads, Glittering Cars

Damaged roads glittering cars
as thick as thieves, helpless policemen,
the business of vendors
getting unprofitable customers got stuck
in a tightened noose.
Unemployment is mushrooming,
overflowing schools and colleges education
getting high-priced pockets getting tight
higher the line of fashion, lower the line of poverty.
Corrupt public
select its own leader, not born from heaven.
How will it be good?
Aging people rising ailments
ailing heart, ailing body.
The journey getting short alienation
from relations deceptive wish
no one besides,
delineation from the new stance
What will one do?
Not the world of humans
emerged a new form
see, how long it remain?
People who create robots should see how they are made.

56. Everyone was immigrant

Everyone was an immigrant,
some were defined; the rest disclosed all
after they left.
The strangers did everything in abundance
to get close to you and us.
After they left
on one was attended.

57. City Vs Village

The city was large,
but the village was small.
A few people in the village,
and he was alone.
Countless people in the city
he was alone.
He was kept isolated by idle talks of the village
and bragging about the city.

58. In my Rajasthan

In my Rajasthan, the rivers get weary
by flowing through the Himalayas.
The clouds get weary while sailing
from the ocean.
The Sun gets weary,
the air gets isolated,
and heaven knows
how much the sky
gets sorrowful
and dries before weeping
and the relief- gets drained
while coming through Delhi.
That never gets weary are the roots
while growing, that never gets weary is the peacock
while dancing, that never gets weary are the trees
and leaves by getting withered, and that never gets weary
are the trees and leaves getting withered
and that never gets weary is the man
in my Rajasthan.

59. Fanaticism

Thy were illusions and
kept on repudiating countless truths.

60. Butterflies

Astonished,
when I became aware of the butterflies
flew far away, traveled across thousand miles
many butterflies, like the birds.

> *Contemplate reasonably these butterflies –*
> *that adore the flowers*
> *dwell with flowers where cleanliness,*
> *greenery and freshness remain*
> *there can we see - butterflies.*

On the highway of the city
the hustle and bustle of the market,
the clutches of people
disease of cleverness
our helplessness in our claws (?)
between the clap-net of others,
I forgot slender the air
exquisite are these - butterflies.

> *Not even a slight negligence that cockroach*
> *will emerge, perhaps won't ruin*
> *thy bread and biscuit don't open the door*
> *and let others enter.*
> *Or else the mosquitoes will suck the blood heedful,*
> *by saving thyself else due to the radiance of home*
> *won't invade some moths.*
> *Didn't ever hear*

that a butterfly stings.
Butterflies don't obtain anything from flowers.
It never happens that butterflies flew
after obtaining nectar from flowers
and in its memory
- the flower withers.
What should we do?
It can't happen;
instead of this
these butterflies will come home.
Many butterflies remain outside
a thousand miles away.
Are these butterflies extinct?
Or these butterflies won't fly across thousand miles.
If not fly inside the homes,
why can't we get a glimpse of - butterflies outside?

61. Departing From Here

Departing from here
When I return
I won't greet you.
It seems,
I won't start asking you for my own address.
Unafraid of losing myself.
I fear losing you in the meanwhile.

62. One Secret

Life doesn't end on this road
can't be straight, always on turns.
This road won't end by reaching one city.
There are numerous cities ahead of it, small and large.
Not true every man residing in a large city
is happier than those in the countryside.
This road
though not straight
leads to many cities.

63. Struggle

The whole day
blazing walls and roofs,
these homes
emitting heat throughout the night
relentlessly, persistently heaven knows
When will these homes be cold?

64. I started Liking her

When
I started liking her.
She was heartbroken
that I am perturbed.
To reduce the distance of the liking
and disliking, I lost myself
by being shrunk
then, by losing oneself
to whom would I lay hands?

65. Prayer

God
I am unaware
What is salvation, and how does it happen?
Perhaps my confrontation with enslavement,
obstacle and agony remained incomplete.
But, I discern
that breaths can be
taken in a more open space.
Oh, God!
When tired, agitated, and stumbled
beyond the efforts I uttered
for salvation.
I can fathom
not everyone,
but
Why some paupers
start asking – alms straightforwardly?

66. Desires

Loose appetite but not thirst
let something have perished
let something befall
desires too are
crucial for life.

EVOKE

Translation Work of Dr. Manish Goswami's book "Do Ladkiyan."

(Two Girls)

67. ….. At Last

He – At last
declared not to be a slave.
The shackles he felt were broken
……….. and thus
got absolute freedom.
There is no absolute freedom,
said some philosophers
but I say………..
"if one walks on a thin pathway,
felt free from shackles
considered as – absolute free".

68. Certainty in Uncertainty

In the uncertainty of things,
if anything is certain – It's you.
Job, land, house, place, and city
nothing is long-lasting
certain is – God.
Not certain for the river where to go,
where to flow swiftly, where to slow,
the only thing certain to forge ahead.
Education makes – Literate not gives the certainty of job
decency – is certain for a literate
not certain to become – a millionaire.
Righteousness – is certain of a righteous
yet does not certain anything, not money, not even body,
and mind, even if that remains barely fine, but the mind of
a righteous – never waves.
Certain for an honest not to be encircled by the troubles
which encircle – the dishonest in uncertainty.
The certainty of having a baby boy has made the life
of innumerable daughters – uncertain, yet the joys were not
certain associated with the birth of a baby boy.
Killed the rights of many poor by brooding
over our own poverty
yet uncertain for a merchant and politician
in which country and condition will be fostered
their grandson and the great-grandson and

to bring you into this world,
my own existence became uncertain.

69. No One.........who Wandered

No regret if the age passes away
for searching home.
Wandered when moved out of the home,
but no one wandered while returning home.
Father –
searching for the best house for us,
got wandered
I, too, forgot his wandering
while wandering for my our children.
Wandering did not take it as-
yet the home will not be
in the corner or edge of the world,
one remains in the center.

70. The House Speaks

My brother!
Even after many years
I failed to become your home.
The house regrets and speaks.
Fool! Please don't sell it - house speaks,
my father poured blood
instead of water in its mud mortar.
You Shameless!
You made it STD-PCO - house speaks
mother reiterated father made it for our comfort.
In dignity, you speak
my brother is pleased
to pay huge money for the house
but, Is the reason to be happy?
You don't have a
heart of stone that ever sells me, and by the way
sleep on the footpath with a bag of money after selling me.
How foolish this man is!
Speak the houses among themselves.
The onion potatoes will
not get costly
if he overlaid us.
The house speaks
how clever this contractor is
who calls me a house

but considers me a shop.
And steps of generations move towards the center.

71. Roof

One
Sky – A roof
God bestowed upon every man
still, a man wished for another one.
Two
Almost everyone should have a roof,
either his own or on rent.
Three
didn't matter
the roof belonged to us
or others
but remained glorious
till father was there.
Four
Flats in lakhs, bungalows in millions
in a rented house or hut,
the roof remains overhead, but these days
very less we stand on our own roof.
Five
In the word of wafers,
will not forget to make potato chips on the roof.
Six
On the roof, we will meet the moon
with the moon, we will meet the stars…
life will exist on a star

where we will meet the parted souls.

72. Oh! Regret?

Have not seen their wings
airplanes declare rockets as handicapped.
Neither talks to rockets
nor expresses thoughts on any level.
Whenever happened to meet,
Airplanes narrated the stories of the sky.
Felt bored after some time,
Airplanes decided to go on the Ozone layer
for an excursion.
The meeting was held for this
felt regret for rockets at first
and then extensive discussions held
for various solutions
to remove the problem of disabled rockets.
Greater in number,
the Airplanes also thought of as charity
to conduct an "Air show" for lesser rockets.
Afterward, discussion was carried out to challenge
the Ozone layer.
After sometime Airplanes
returned from a stroll to
the Ozone Layer.
The Rockets were also resting
but Ah! Airplanes didn't know.
Meanwhile,

these few rockets came back
after a stroll from the moon.

73. Cheat

When I will cover your eyes with my fingers
and show you the world
through the sticky pictures on them,
Will you consider it a truth?
But when you see the real world
through the space of my fingers
my existence will remain no more then.
Except for my deceiving fingers
you will not see anything after that.

74. Two Girls

Two girls,
Keeping hand in hand, dancing.
Father, you stand; we dance,
And then you will see
You will start dancing on your own.
Father scared — "see, the bushes don't dance a lot —
see! How crowded is it
don't get hurt by someone's nail."
Father scared — but two girls flying in the sky
keeping a hand in hand
"Father, just stand like this and see we fly;
you will fly on your own."
Father scared —
Saying stop, wait, don't fly
You didn't ever go to the sky.
The wind is hot; weird clouds don't fly
scared father but two girls running and jumping
"Father, you sit, and we go outside."
Father scared — 'stop, wait,' saying that,
but two girls show
walking on the rope keeping the foot
on the head of the crowd saying to father
See this! See this!
by becoming the spring of the forest
falling from the fear of father,

again becoming a cloud came down
from the sky
Two fairies become the bride
leaving the father's house.
Two girls hurriedly came to
make their father sits on the wings
for sightseeing scared father
Oh! You will fall so heavy I am
this is not a custom, not a right thing."
Father saying this
"Oh! Look around; what people will say."
Father scared
Father scared.

75. House: Ours or Rented....

"We will move from here; we will move from here,"
and father stayed in one place for years.
House prices skyrocketed in these years,
but we stayed on rent.
"I will not go will not go
I will stay here for quite a long."
I thought of this in my first job
for building a house,
I bought a land
but shifted suddenly to some other city
which was near to father.
"Now we all will stay here
and will not go anywhere
surely will stay here."
Then What?
But Father shifted to another world
Or don't know where.....
and I, too, shifted
in another city in rented accommodation........

76. Apology

An unintentional small mistake could be forgiven
The unintentional mistake was too big to come
in the category of an apology.
He was standing, sagging his mouth,
Saying -"Give me punishment,
Give me punishment,"
but a voice came from somewhere
"What punishment does he deserve?
Leave it"
Perhaps this was his biggest punishment.

77. Its Morning

It is dawn the loudspeakers of Temples,
Mosques and Gurudwaras
have officially announced
the continuous existence of their God
and started issuing the entry letter
in the form of flowers, joss sticks, and slips…
It is dawn
the chirping of the remaining birds is coming.
In the park, the fast footsteps formed a balance
between mobile, ears, and tongue.
The milkman collected the freshwater;
the distant scantily scattered greenery in the city,
in the garden from the polythene of garbage.
The Striving plants bloomed, surprised and
saying, "see! Ah! we bloomed
Oh! It is morning!!!".....
Mother forced their children to go to the washroom
then, ladies wearing nighties,
lazy drivers
looking at well-dressed children,
realizing the fragrance of hair oil, it is morning.
Besides inflation, during the last financial
year, grandfather's retirement FD got doubled.
Till now, many grandfather's friends fallen into slumber,
but the survived grandfather feels that

this morning will give birth to many glorious mornings.
Restless throughout the night with sips of tea
made himself comprehend it is morning........
Staying in one job as an assured professional
lifted a newspaper
with a cup of tea and read a quotation.
"In the corporate sector,
you should change the job
only if you are ensconced
and good at your current job."
And oh! the assured
baffled in the early morning
then his morning to change the job
has come.
In paradise...........
after the report of the inspection committee,
Bramha Ji decided,
However, we need to arrange
a new kind of morning on earth.

78. A Statement: Not a poem

I am talking here about wearing good spectacles.
Please consider it mere spectacles, not my stance
Don't be deceived
by wearing good shoes and the energy
to be used for steps.
I am talking here about wearing clean, stainless clothes.
Please don't attach it with a reflection
I am talking here of pure spectacles, shoes, clothes
and want to say without snatching it from someone,
come and try to make it all better.

79. Reality of dreams – Life or reality of life – A Dream

Suddenly, it started happening,
what he had perceived,
Surmised, he felt that and experienced
a hundred percent anticipated the impending
and in a millionth of a second,
it materialized – just for some minutes
and for a while, exactly as he thought,
he felt – Is he witnessing an old dream – in reality,
or this reality itself is a dream just like that.

80. Need

Since birth, I found father has fewer needs;
we always had more while we already
had more – from him……..

81. Thy be Lord Krishna

Thy be a deity,
I be love
a devotee be our bond,
not essential for a devotee
righteously love forever
and when weary in love,
the devotee bond uses his privilege
the love continues..........
Thy be Krishna,
I be Mira
not essential Krishna eternally
embodied the form of male,
Let – I be Mira.
Or thy be a bumble bee,
I be fragrance
our bond be a flower
dazzling, unwavering, refreshing, and blooming
I be scattered
come as a naughty bumble bee.
Let I be fragrance.
Let I be fragrance; thy be profound
I be the stream,
let thy be ocean
this time, I take stride thy rest
even if the world builds a bridge upon me

I be clouds,
thy be as ample as the ground
I turn into rain
this time……..
Let thy be the ocean; I be the stream.

82. It is Life

Not an arrow that hits its mark precisely,
It is life that rather has a
the promise of exceptional shot.
At times, even after the shot won't be told
to come and move heaven and earth once more,
It is life, here targets change like seasons, harvests,
shores of streams, and as shades of clouds….
Not an equation once unravelled
the answer can't be refined.
It is the life that offers an answer
to the very equation
to know the wholly disparate answer.
…………..An unsolved riddle,
Kept for months in the wait to be solved………
it seems a man evaluating himself less
when ready to leave
woke up suddenly from sleep
and saw it solved in different threads,
swathe itself in organized bundles of life
was just a riddle like that.

83. Inchmeal

Slowly and steadily, month by month,
instalments by instalments
we owned the house.......
Bit by bit, year by year,
interest by interest
becoming the crook of old age
my provident fund......
In a few years, inch by inch
this tyre, this seat, this handle, this tank
will slide from the finance company's right,
and this motorcycle will become – my own.
Step by step, month by month,
materialistic things
are becoming my right.
But, gradually, second by second
mine leaving this world
is on the verge.
....
.... The Banyan tree, by degrees
did not fathom how its main trunk got dropped
........inchmeal when hundreds of branches
transmuted into the trunk after enrooted,
clinging it......
........yet not vigilant
.......The Banyan tree.

84. On being Women

Ever she kept it in mind
a man is a man
and a woman, a woman.
When she got an equal status to a man
Whilst proceeding and advancing
and at someplace
no question was there
to be compared
with the woman or with the man
she then felt so proud of being a woman…..

85. Did the World Change?

We altered the world then,
altered our own world
afterwards, changed ourselves,
atop that, we altered our façade through expressions.
We reformed everything.
Just don't get stuck
it is the symbol of stagnation.
We kept on changing, considering it permanent.
When we didn't find any change,
we solely changed the symbol
to justify that;
said – change.
To unchange, to stagnant
and stagnation meant – lifelessness
rather wanted to be exuberant merciless,
spiritless, callous
we changed the perception.
A hero husband kept the same love
just changed the wife
a wife kept the same husband
just change her love
and.....
didn't change the facade, change the inner man.

86. Introspection

Slowly he shut the door
not apprehensive of outdoor lights,
dismayed by guests
or afraid of noise.
Not strayed naked at home,
he still shuts the windows and
slowly drew all the curtains.
Not being fascinated to say anything
while sharing lessens the heat of agonizing pain.
Sharing hurtful things with near and dear ones
lessen its impact like a burning amber would lose its fire,
cool down and turn to ash; perhaps it was not a thing –
When shared remained less heated,
he just wanted to sink in himself.
Though had complaints from outer, perhaps
not intended to share or show wisdom
in believing it pointless to speak.
He can be innocent and
considered outer a devil.....
by mistake.
Actually, what happened was,
he closed all windows and doors
and drew curtains and…
slowly and steadily getting overlooked,
it became an empty house.

None came to the house; neither peeped nor saw.
Friends and people thought and said
by looking at the seemed closed house, "perhaps he went out."
while it was such a closed house
where he was a hundred percent present
and by the absence of others and detached,
departed from the vicinity
away, and far away......

87. The First Human

The first human evolved from an animal
surprised at his success in evolution.
The first human was extremely delighted
with his success in the evolutionary chain.
Leapt and jumped in the sky,
went to his mother with the news he stood "First."
Mother's joys knowing no bounds
As her son was ------ "The First Human."
The first human still somewhere survived, in the present;
felt regretted didn't become a merchant,
religious contractor, intellectual, psychophant,
and backbiter
didn't acquire anything, nothing............
The first human
full of self – condemnation
came to his mother
"uttering and lamenting
I didn't become anything."
Bizarre voices came from the vicinity saying -----
"Keep your inner animal alive --- The First Human."
But, the mother could not allow herself to break
the trophy of --- "The First Human."
The mother also knew this -----
the first human won't be nurtured throughout life
in the shade of mother's handholding rather

keeping faith in the capabilities of the son,
the mother encouraged her to look for
the first land, the first sky like her own.
The mothers of these first humans
had the same trust in the initiative of their sons
as they had ------
on the first human evolved from an animal.

88. The one

Beyond the grip of words means that we call 'he';
he is not him.
It has neither any boundary nor any direction.
"It is ahead of our thinking" there is nothing
as it has no speed. But it doesn't mean it is still.
Actually, it is beyond definition.
It is beyond every colossal and every profound,
but it is something
it is beyond any existence
it is beyond the existence of beyond.
Perhaps it says
we are so small that
it is beyond consideration.
We should not think about what is the Universe
or if we are in the milky way and the milky way
is in the Universe,
then where is the Universe?
And wherever the Universe is,
Then, where is He in that?
He tells us about thinking of this and says
it is not our work to think of it.
If we are stable and resonating in us
thus, which is so colossal outside,
still minute inside.
By being the same inside out,

he says but speaks nothing
as he is beyond comprehension or
to comprehend.
He is in us, or we are in Him.

89. I and the labourer

Labourer picked a piece of sweet in his hands;
Mouth- watered
labourer rejoiced, felt mirth jubilated it
overwhelmed by eating sweets –
Got sweets! Got sweets!
I, too, thought of gaiety
likewise filled pockets,
went to market, bought enough sweets
I ate a lot! Ate a lot! and ate a lot!
but nothing peculiar befallen
didn't touch Labourer's
equivalent ecstasy,
his paralleled bliss
I yearned for that sweetness!
That sweetness! that sweetness!

90. Evoke

From the cage of the butcher – the cock,
gives a prayer call
"get up; It's morning".
From the cage of the butcher,
the cock awakens those in slumber
with zeal and said
"You slothful, get up and
enjoy the morning
and feel yourself – unconfined! "

www.ingramcontent.com/pod-product-compliance
Lightning Source LLC
Chambersburg PA
CBHW021548150726
47990CB00006B/2454